Telephone Man

Dear Helen,

It's a pleasure to be your fellow "poet of warp & weft"! With great admiration for your spirit & work, warmly, Mary Ann

Poems

Mary Ann Mayer

(and Bob Maitland who you would have enjoyed and he, you.)

authorHOUSE™

1663 LIBERTY DRIVE, SUITE 200
BLOOMINGTON, INDIANA 47403
(800) 839-8640
WWW.AUTHORHOUSE.COM

First published by AuthorHouse 12/12/05

ISBN: 1-4208-7971-5 (sc)

Library of Congress Control Number: 2005907788

Printed in the United States of America
Bloomington, Indiana

This book is printed on acid-free paper.

Book design and photography by Carl Peter Mayer

Front cover painting by Bruce Mitchell
Also West of 810 Farmington Ave. (detail)
Rear cover painting by Bruce Mitchell
5 to the West

Credit Line: "Men In The Sky", from *Different Hours*
By Stephen Dunn. Copyright @ 2000 by Stephen Dunn.
Used by permission of W.W. Norton & Company, Inc.

Library of Congress Cataloging-in-Publication Data...
Mayer, Mary Ann
Telephone man: poems / Mary Ann Mayer

The poems in this book are from the stories of
my father, Bob Maitland

and are dedicated with love, to him

My phone
is ringing. It's one of the telephone men,
the highest, the one with a sufficiency
of tools around his waist, calling to see
if everything's all right.

Stephen Dunn, *Men In The Sky*

Contents

Telephone Man

Out of the Foxhole

I couldn't work inside
after the war
though I liked the machine shop
and Potter & Johnson
kept my job open
running the Warner-Swayze turret lathe
I was good at it
so after the war I went back for a while
threading screws making bolts by the thousand
but felt cooped up, closed in
is how I recall it
no   I never thought stars
could look so bright
from the trench
as they did
and that I could breathe
easiest in the holes
I dug out in coral on Biak Island
never deep
always with a ledge to grab on to
          in forty-five
I was relieved to hear
the phone company was hiring
I put my name in
got my ladder truck soon after that
and spent the next thirty-seven years
outside   climbing

Class Education

I ring the doorbell
telephone man   I say
she opens the door a crack
you can't come in here
I can't let you in the front door
there's a door around the back
now be a nice man and walk around
go in the back way
what would the neighbors think
seeing a tradesman come in my front door?

Cuttin Out

strap on your climbers
cinch the band around your boot
then around each ankle and calf
grab the pole
jab in one boot
stand up and lock your knee
jab in the other boot
lean back and climb
remember never to straighten up
or you'll be on the ground lookin up
cuttin out's bad
I did twice   slipped six feet
arms loaded with creosote and splinters
from huggin the pole
one time hornets flyin out of the terminal box
chased me down
the other time those bloody blue jays
nesting on the cross-arm ten feet above my head
diving pecking my hard-hat
all the way down the pole
they chased me half a mile up the street
I ran past Oak Grove Cemetery
all the way to pole 23
at Industrial Highway crossing Central Ave

Safety Exam

one time a year the safety supervisor
would ride with you for a couple of hours
so Gene was ridin with me
and we're drivin down past the hot wienie joints
on Dexter   past Sparky's opposite Stanley's
and I could tell he was scared
he said   Jesus Christ Bob
do you drive like this all the time?
I can't put my hand between your truck
and that parked car
I can't take this Bob bring me back to the garage
will ya?

Heater Fan

I still hear it
that tin sound
the day John was ridin with me
to a two-man job
I never thought he'd do it
I was drivin the ladder truck
the thirty-seven Ford with the ladder hung
on the driver's side blocking the door
John said   Bob we're not gettin any heat
I said   John maybe the fan isn't on
put your hand down there see if it's running
but I never thought he'd do it
I thought he was just making believe doin it
when he reached down to the floor
under the glove compartment
put his hand on the fan
in back of the heater
and I'll never forget how
I had to crawl over him to get out
and get him out too
bleedin like a son of a gun
at the corner of Cross and Broad

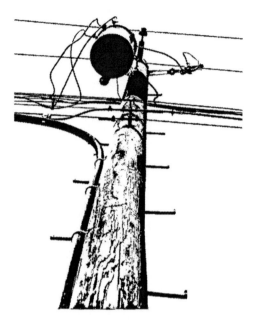

Steppin the Pole

climb the pole four feet with your spikes
reach to seven feet and
drill a three-quarter inch hole
pound in a twelve-inch iron step
with the blunt end of your hand ax
keep goin   drillin holes   poundin steps
every eighteen inches
on opposite sides of the pole
all the way up

that's what the linemen did
before '52
when they were settin new poles
but after '52
they stopped steppin the poles because
kids were climbin up and fallin off
getting hurt
so on the new poles with no steps we had to
spike up with climbers to get to the job
shift your weight to rest
when your legs were goin numb
from havin your knees locked
and all your weight on the spikes
you'd never know until you got out to the job
if you'd be lucky
to get a stepped pole
either way   steps or no steps
climbin wasn't easy
whoever said
the longer you work the job
the easier it gets
didn't hear that our bucket-trucks came in
two weeks after I retired

Wire Chief

he's in charge of everyone who works outside
but he never called me on anything
except once
he got me good over near Prospect Heights
he liked us to pull all the wires up tight
but not too tight   leave some play in 'em
he liked the wires close together
hangin with just the right amount of slack
nice and neat so they look like all one cable
he saw a job I did   thought I left too much sag
called me into his office and said
that job should bring a blush of shame to your face

Iron Lung

when I walked into the living room I heard a racket
even before I saw her layin there
like she was in a casket   her head stickin out one end
sealed off around the neck with a rubber gasket

it sounded like a machine shop
the way the pumps and compressors drown everything out
so when I heard
hello
I jumped
then felt so bad
it must've been a big effort for her
she must've seen me first
in the mirror tilted over her head
before I saw her

as I remember she was forty-five or fifty
I've often thought about that lady and wished
I'd hung around and talked to her
I guess she could talk   I was installin her phone
but maybe she wouldn't want to
I coulda found out I suppose
ask her if she wanted anything
I remember I was thinkin   and I'm not kiddin
maybe someone could bring her some ear plugs

My Foreman

Russell was a nice enough guy
but strictly by the book
he was Mr. Bell you know what I mean?
he was Alexander's cousin alright
so Russell drives out to find me on a job
all the way out in Lincoln near Sam's drug store
he wouldn't take any guff   I knew that
so I didn't give him any
when I had to go back with him to the last job I'd done
all the way over on Armistice boulevard
just to move a damn cleat two inches
it was the final cleat I'd put up
to hold the wire to the roof rafter
and he'd gone over there and measured the distance
I put it from the fuses   I was eight inches
when the book said five inches
he even showed me the damn page in the book
so I had to move it over three inches
Russell'd come riding around checking on me
        if I put the cone out in back of the truck
        if the wheels were turned in to the curb
and if they weren't he'd get all serious and say
Bob just think what would happen if the truck rolled
Yeah Russell I'd say   it'd roll and then stop
Bob everything's a joke with you
you're a nice enough guy
without the guff

Dream Job

one girl in the coin department
who counted the coins
that the guys who emptied the coin boxes
collected and turned in
admitted to stealin hundreds of dollars
for years stuffin the coins in her bra

I asked for a transfer to that coin department
right away
I offered to take a fifty percent pay cut
I told 'em
I thought they might need me to find the stolen money
I often wonder why I didn't get the transfer

Hand in the Till

I knew a lot of guys
who'd chance it
fact I know one guy
got caught red-handed

management was lookin for guys on the take
        so one day they planted money
jammed the coin chute with coins
then told test board to send this guy out
to fix the trouble

so when he goes out to clear the chute
gets the coins out
then drops them back in like he's supposed to
while the operator keeps count
well he doesn't put it all back in
tells the operator he put it all in
then they had him   red-handed
with ten dollars under his floor mat

some guys did it for years without gettin caught
I mean *before* they got caught
cuz they could watch you for years
just to catch you with your hand in the till
thinkin the whole time you were gettin away with it
they'd catch you eventually   believe me

not that I didn't think about it myself sometimes

Somethin for Nothin

everybody's got a phone
everybody wants somethin for nothin
so when you're a phone man
everybody's always asking
got any rolls of tape Bob?
got an extra phone?
got a longer cord?
got a shorter cord?
got a black cord?
got a white cord?
how 'bout off-white?
got a wall plate?
got an extra jack? I could use another extension
got a little time on the weekend to help me put it in?
that's not a lot of work is it Bob?
hey what else you got on the truck?
it ain't like stealin'
it's a big company right?

Cable Repair

725-6627   there's a short on your line
trouble could be anywhere around here
up any side street
find it fix it
725-6627 is an orange-white pair
in a blue-white binder
splice those wires
twenty-two gauge
in a hundred pair cable
cross 'em spin 'em
put on desiccant to dry the moisture out
wrap it with tape
check the line   dial the number
get a ring back
but I don't need to know your number to ring your line
or to have your line ring me back on top of the pole
I just need to know your colors

New Kid

the new kid
reports to the cable department
his cousin yells to the mechanic
standing next to the time clock
hey Stan it's my cousin Dick's first day
Stan looks up   flips the kid the bird
Mike the foreman comes in from the cable yard
his cousin goes
hey Mike it's my cousin Dick's first day
Mike slaps the kid on the side of the head
your cousin don't have the brains he was born with
geez now I got two of ya
      kid move yer skinny ass
go tell Helen in the office we need more hand cream
yeah that's it   we're outta hand cream
and don't let the door hit ya in the ass

Blue Princess

it was a sixteenth birthday present
from her mother and father
I remember wantin to rush to install it
and get outta there before she came home
from school   so she'd be surprised
on her birthday
so I'm backin outta their driveway
when Mrs. Berard runs to the door and yells
President Kennedy was just shot!
and I was on my way to Moran's house
to install a jack in the upstairs bedroom
spent the next three hours there watchin TV
when I got back to the garage nobody said a thing
about spendin all day on
one princess
and a jack

Settin Poles

five guys on the truck   our line gang
loaned to Vermont after heavy wet snow
up there they set their poles
only three feet deep   instead of six feet
like we set 'em down here   so they tumbled over
the wires snapped under the weight of snow and ice
pulled the poles right out of the ground
and in the middle of the job Denelle my house builder
calls from Pawtucket to ask me
to come back to pass papers December twenty-fourth
on our new house on Denson Road
he wanted me home before the end of the year
for his tax purposes
he was gonna bring the papers up to Vermont
for me to sign if I couldn't get home
I got home

Morning Sickness

before our first baby
two   three months
almost every day
the same thing
my truck pulled over
at pole 3
on my way to the garage
every morning same pole
on Promenade Street
I'd crouch in the weeds
throwing up
bran flakes and Sanka
I really didn't know why
it was happening at the time
not 'til after   two babies born
and that story never got out
down at the garage
Dot swore she wouldn't tell
boy I'd never live that one down

Takin a Dump

Maitland   can't ya take a dump at home
like everybody else?
is it too much to ask
to goddamn get here on time
and that don't mean eight o'clock
punch in then go to the can for half an hour
I mean eight sharp sittin in your truck
y'understand?
        hey John   maybe you got a faucet
with a shut-off on yours
but I don't got one on mine

S.O.B.

Dave was promoted to foreman
we had a meeting in the room
just the twelve men
he thought he knew it all
talked real fast
said he'd be out to check on the guys
and if anything's wrong he said
I'll tell ya but I won't ride your case cuz
I'm your friend first and want to help you
in every possible way
not have you think I'm a sonofabitch
so I yell out   hey Dave
I thought that fact had already been established!
he got so hot under the collar
he didn't know whether to shit or go blind
the guys they all fell off their chairs laughin
that was the best part of it
he couldn't stand me after that

Recon

five of us were on a loan to 'Gansett
driving behind Frank the trouble foreman
when he decides to pull his truck over
and call a safety meeting
it was a hot day hundred degrees in the shade
we're sittin under a tree and I decide to climb the tree
Frank was readin the safety regulations
he stopped   looked around   wondering where
Maitland went
looks up and sees me sittin on a branch
he got tearin   what the hell are you doin up there?
how the hell do ya think that looks?
I'm runnin a safety meeting
and you fall out of a tree?

Barbell

just the other day goin
to Pawtucket Memorial Hospital to pay a bill
I pass White Street
and thirty years later it dawns on me
gee that's the house where I had to get out fast
run away from a guy   a body builder
he was all muscle
he lived to make muscle
and wanted you to know it   that type
cripes he had fingers bigger than my thighs
his basement was loaded with barbells
and he's watchin me fix a trouble
kinda breathin down my neck   so I look around
at all the iron weights
I look him up and down
cripes he had muscles comin out his ears
I said   so these your kid's weights?
he said   they're mine
I said   boy you'd never know it
I tell ya he was tearin and he ran upstairs and started
throwin things and screamin at his wife
I got outta there fast
I was glad I was all done fixin the trouble
and *could* get out
cuz he woulda killed me

34

Wiring Point Judith

I was loaned to the line gang
and all winter in the bitter cold
we ran cable
ran one hundred pair two miles
hands freezin working in gloves with no fingers
I climbed every third pole on Point Judith Road
and down the Escape Road
to the water at Great Island
another crew took it from there
laid it underwater
I remember lunch at
George's of Galilee
how the heat slammed you first
how good that felt
then the chowder

Shakedown at the Track

I was workin in the bar room at the end of Broad
and in comes Bill   he was a wheel
and he said   Maitland drop everything
we have to meet the FBI and the head of the legal
department up at Lincoln Downs
I said   but Bill I got this fuse box here all apart
well   he said   throw it back together
give' em service and let's get outta here

the feds were after somebody broadcasting the races
from the horse track to a bookie joint in Boston
they figured it out because the phone was a two-party line
and one party was the Clover Leaf motel across town
somebody got wind of it in the motel
heard a race called when they picked up the phone

I had to go find the other phone
so they gave me the pole numbers
where the line connected
between Cobble Hill and Louisquisett Pike
I climbed three or four poles then I found it
traced the line into a cottage right next door
to Mama's spaghetti joint
I tapped in   listened to 'em call the race

they're off and runnin on the rail at the second turn
the track is fast here in Lincoln Downs
it's Blue Socks in front...

from up the pole I signaled 'em
waved and pointed to the cottage
instead the FBI men go runnin up to Mama's
and bust down the door   I'm yellin to 'em that
they're at the wrong place
the bunch of jerks didn't listen
they must've thought I was a dope
they finally got it right and stormed the cottage

but nobody's in there   nobody needed to be   turns out
from *that* phone someone had run a drop wire half a mile
out to a barn at the back stretch of the track
where a guy in the hay loft with binoculars
is watchin the race through a cut-out in the eaves
callin results down
to a twenty-two year old kid from South Providence
hiding behind the hay bales manning the phone

after the feds nabbed them
I coiled up two-thousand feet of drop wire
worked all night in front of my truck headlights
got stuck in the mud

Funny How

funny how
some people can't take a joke
I pull up next to a guy at the red light
corner of South Bend and Division
in back of McCoy Stadium
and he's pickin his nose I tell ya
he's up to his knuckles
pickin and diggin like no tomorrow
anyway it's a long light and I'm lookin
down at him from my truck
goin at it   then I start to copy him
and beep my horn
so he'll look up and get a laugh
when he sees me pickin too
I yell over to him   hey pal save me one
but when he does look up
boy oh boy
I swear to god
he's madder n' a wet hen
ya never seen anybody so mad
screamin out the window
I'm darn lucky
I got the green

In Pulaski Square

two women in a tenement
arguing
one on the second floor landing
one on the third floor landing
screams
I'll tell ya right now that isn't your kid
that's livin with you
and she throws
a head of cabbage down the stairs
hits the other one in the head with it
I turned around and walked out the door
waited an hour
before going back in

Ear Wax

old ladies in particular
would call for a repair
say they can't hear
       you know why they can't hear?
the little holes in the receiver would be
filled up with ear wax
caked with the stuff
you wouldn't believe how thick
       but you can't insult 'em
so when they ask   what's the trouble sir?
I'd just tell 'em I fixed it
a corroded wire was all

Kinds of Troubles

no dial tone?   could be all kinds of reasons
why you're not getting dial tone
short in the cable or someone hit a pole half-a-mile away

cross-talk?   pick up your phone and you overhear
someone down the road at Larry's Gulf station
that's wet wires in the cable   shorted to another phone

customer can't hear a caller or a caller can't hear them?
mouth-piece caked with food and spit
I couldn't tell 'em it smelled like someone threw up in it
I'd just unscrew it and say you got somethin in there you
might want to wash it   customer'd be surprised

blown fuses from lightning storms is how
I got into all the mansions in Newport
if one fuse blew   dispatcher would tell me
        Bob go change the fuses in all the houses
on the street jes to be on the safe side

other kinds of troubles? oh there's
bad transmitter   bad receiver   bad cord
and static?
water'd get into the old woven asbestos coating and
corrode the copper   I could sniff out corroded wires
guys couldn't get over it
I'd look up and see green in the splice in the drop-wire

coming from the terminal overhead
goin into the house fuses
I'd whack that drop-wire with my tree-trimmer
and get the static goin
clip my test set into the wire right on the house
and confirm it right there
find the trouble
I saved myself a lot of climbin

Cat House

diagonally across from
Matteo the tailor
in the brown three-decker
thirty cats if there was one
were livin in the cellar
and it stunk
but I did the job anyway
gawd I felt sorry for the lady
she was built like a brick shithouse
gland trouble probably
and too big to do the stairs
a few years later there was a fire there
and I'm talkin to a lieutenant on the squad
told him I did a job in that house once
he said I hope you didn't have to work in the attic
where she kept her dogs

Dodgin Shit

in a tenement behind the New York Lace Store
all the turds come ploppin down
whenever they flush upstairs
landin right beside me
on the cellar floor
workin on the fuses
because
the darn sewer pipe is disconnected
I gotta dodge turds

A Limit to Service

m'am
why do you want me to take my shoes off?
even in my own house
I don't take off my shoes
besides they're clean
and I'm just doing your inside repair
I won't be dragging dirt in so
no I can't take off my shoes
I'll call my boss
have him send somebody else out
to do the job
the new guy
might take off his shoes

Filth

I had to move the customer's sofa
to get to the jack in the mop board
and when I pulled the sofa out
there was a dozen banana peels
dirty underwear
apple cores
everything
under that sofa
she saw all the junk
said   I'm sorry
I had an emergency
and haven't had a chance to clean today

On Garfield Street

across from the police station
two women livin on the second floor
with a kid 'bout five years old
he comes out of his room with no clothes on
and one of them says   Jimmy
get back in there and stop showin off
the telephone man has a bigger one than you

Charity Begins at Home

my throwin arm was good
so the Pawtucket Times kept me on
delivering before school
I'd throw each newspaper
from my bicycle
up on to every porch on Sweet
and half of Suffolk
my aim
was so good
I never even braked or got off my bike
to run up the steps
or fish one out of the shrubs
I was the only paperboy
on the Darlington route
some customers tipped two cents a week
I had four blocks of jickies, polaks,
frenchies and micks
and I had to be nice to all of em
       Mum made sure I knew
she'd hear about it if I wasn't
she wouldn't let me charge
certain ones if they were having hard times
made me pay for their paper outta my tips

so when Mrs. Boba stopped the paper
after her husband died
I still pedaled by her house   slow
just in case she changed her mind
because even if you're sad
so long as you're alive
news is good
right?

Tools

voltmeter around your neck
test set clipped on your belt
canvas tool bag hangin on your belt
next to rolls of tape hittin you in the rear
while you're climbin   loaded down
with d-rings cutters cable-ties crimps and connectors
a can of hornet spray near full if you're lucky
cuz once you're up there you're at their mercy
and it's a good idea
to take your hand ax and whack the pole before goin up
give 'em warning   then you can get up to the job
unhook the d-ring on your body belt
swing the belt around the pole
hook it on the other hip
lean back   relax   hope
you didn't forget
your Lucky Strikes and matches in the truck
kids'd be lookin up watchin ya the whole time
the set-up   the climb   the sun
hitting your spikes and tools high up there
one ear cupping the test set against your shoulder
two hands cupping a match to light your smoke
they yell   hey phone man   hey phone man
then   you give 'em what they're waiting for
a wave down to those upturned faces

Bob Maitland 1974

Afterword: Bob's Daughter Remembers Driving Lessons

dad couldn't cuss worth his salt
or insult anybody even if they needed it
he wouldn't even say goddamn
even though the guys at the garage
were world class cussers
and he heard it all in spades
he'd tell us   and he meant it
that if we can't say something nice about someone
don't say anything at all
we didn't buy it   my sister and me
but in dad's mind nobody was a loser

especially the little guy
always root for the little guy he'd say
the underdog   the one somebody else
is calling loser
then to make his point
he'd stop the car on Jenckes Hill
on our way to buy ice cream cones
pull over beside the white corral
and point out two horses
see that frisky white stallion he'd say
that beauty prancing around and everybody watching?
now see that mangy brown mare alone in the corner?
if you could have one, which horse would you pick?

every time he'd answer his own question
why the down and out one is always
the good horse   cuz looks don't mean anything
it's not that dad was milk toast exactly
he'd get burned up sometimes
and the one thing that rubbed him the wrong way
was somebody mouthing off like a big shot
that guy's a big-I-am he'd say
see   dad knew when he was being taken
for a little guy   for a working stiff
dad sure knew how to teach

Acknowledgment

Robert Leo Maitland, also known as Bob or Leo, was born in 1919 in Pawtucket (Darlington), Rhode Island. He was an installer-repairman for New England Telephone from 1945 until retiring in 1982. These poems are written in his voice, which I hope will delight friends and strangers alike. The content of these poems is not factual, merely true. In most cases, names have been changed.

My father has never called himself a poet, not even a story teller, although he was. He kept his ear to the wire, made imaginative connections, and had a great lyrical memory. With his straightforward, compelling voice, he sure could deliver a line and humor the truth.

With his yen for the road and the quirks in things as well as people, my father came home from work each day full of stories. In hindsight, I believe he came home a satisfied man.

He met my mother, Dorothy Walsh, while she was working as a teletype operator at the phone company.
They married in 1952. They haven't stopped talking.

About The Author

Mary Ann (Maitland) Mayer grew up in Lincoln, Rhode Island. She has practiced occupational therapy for twenty-five years and began writing poetry ten years ago. Her poems have appeared in several journals and anthologies. She is a past recipient of a Massachusetts Cultural Council award. Mary Ann is proud that *Telephone Man* is her first book of poetry. She considers the opportunity to collaborate with her father and to render his experiences into poems, a gift. About *Telephone Man*, she says: Although the diction and images of this book are unique and mark a departure from my usual poetry, I always enjoy imaginatively rendering real experiences, and the grittier the better. I feel that poetry is an ideal way to evoke meaning from the commonplace, and to shine a light into the hidden corners of daily life.

Breinigsville, PA USA
01 March 2011
256563BV00004B/1/A